Contents

Pineapple Orange Walnut Bread

Prep: 20 min.   Bake: 60 min.

2 cups all-purpose flour
1 teaspoon baking powder
½ teaspoon baking soda
¼ teaspoon salt
¼ cup butter **or** margarine,
softened
¾ cup sugar
1 egg

1 tablespoon grated
orange peel
¼ cup orange juice
1 can (8 oz.) DOLE Crushed
Pineapple, undrained
1 cup DOLE Seedless **or**
Golden Raisins
1 cup chopped walnuts,
toasted

- **Combine** flour, baking powder, baking soda and salt in medium bowl; set aside.

- **Beat** together butter and sugar in large bowl until light and fluffy. Beat in egg, orange peel and orange juice. Alternately stir in one-third flour mixture and one-half undrained crushed pineapple until just blended, ending with flour. Stir in raisins and walnuts.

- **Pour** batter into 9 × 5-inch loaf pan sprayed with nonstick vegetable cooking spray.

- **Bake** at 350°F., 60 minutes or until toothpick inserted in center comes out clean. Cool in pan 10 minutes; remove from pan and cool completely on wire rack.

Makes 12 servings

Per Serving: 248 calories, 9g fat (2g sat.), 20mg cholesterol, 177mg sodium, 39g carbohydrate (2g dietary fiber, 23g sugars), 5g protein, 2% Vit A, 9% Vit C, 3% calcium, 10% iron, 6% potassium, 10% folate

BREAKFAST

4

Pineapple Bran Muffins

Prep: 20 min.   Bake: 23 min.

1 can (8 oz.) DOLE
Crushed Pineapple **or**
Pineapple Tidbits
1 cup all-bran cereal
¼ cup milk
½ cup DOLE Seedless **or**
Golden Raisins (optional)
1 egg, slightly beaten

¼ cup vegetable oil
2 tablespoons light **or** dark
molasses
1 cup all-purpose flour
⅓ cup sugar
2 teaspoons baking powder
¼ teaspoon salt

- **Drain** pineapple well, reserve ¼ cup juice.

- **Combine** reserved juice, cereal and milk in large bowl. Let stand a few minutes to soften cereal. Stir in pineapple, raisins, egg, oil and molasses.

- **Combine** flour, sugar, baking powder and salt. Add to pineapple mixture. Stir just to combine.

- **Spoon** batter into 6 (⅔-cup-sized) muffin cups, sprayed with nonstick vegetable cooking spray. Bake at 400°F., 18 to 23 minutes or until toothpick inserted in center comes out clean.

Makes 6 muffins

Per Serving: 273 calories, 11g fat (1g sat.), 32mg cholesterol, 329mg sodium, 44g carbohydrate (4g dietary fiber, 20g sugars), 5g protein, 5% Vit A, 10% Vit C, 10% calcium, 20% iron, 10% potassium, 40% folate

BREAKFAST

5

Pineapple Carrot Raisin Muffins

Prep: 20 min. Bake: 20 min.

2 cups all-purpose flour
1 cup sugar
1½ teaspoons baking powder
1 teaspoon ground cinnamon
1 can (8 oz.) DOLE Crushed
  Pineapple, undrained
2 eggs

½ cup butter **or** margarine,
  melted
1 cup DOLE Seedless **or**
  Golden Raisins
½ cup shredded DOLE
  Carrots

- **Combine** flour, sugar, baking powder and cinnamon in large bowl.

- **Add** undrained pineapple, eggs, butter, raisins and carrots; stir until just blended.

- **Spoon** evenly into 36 mini-muffin cups sprayed with nonstick vegetable cooking spray.

- **Bake** at 375°F., 15 to 20 minutes or until toothpick inserted in center comes out clean. Remove muffins from pans onto wire rack to cool.

For 2½-inch muffins: Spoon batter into 2½-inch muffin pans instead of mini-muffin pans. Bake as directed for 20 to 25 minutes. Cool as directed.

Makes 36 mini-muffins

Per Serving: **73** calories, 2g fat (1g sat.), 13mg cholesterol, 42mg sodium, 14g carbohydrate (0g dietary fiber, 8g sugars), 1g protein, 6% Vit A, 2% Vit C, 2% calcium, 3% iron, 2% potassium, 3% folate

Pineapple Spice Scones

Prep: 20 min.   Bake: 15 min.

2¼ cups all-purpose flour
⅓ cup plus 1 tablespoon
   sugar, divided
2¼ teaspoons baking powder
½ teaspoon baking soda
¼ teaspoon salt
½ cup butter **or** margarine,
   softened

1 can (8 oz.) DOLE Crushed
   Pineapple, undrained
1 teaspoon vanilla extract
   Milk **or** cream
3 tablespoons almonds, finely
   chopped
½ teaspoon ground cinnamon

- **Combine** flour, ⅓ cup sugar, baking powder, baking soda and salt in mixing bowl. Stir to combine. Cut in butter with pastry blender until mixture resembles coarse crumbs. Make well in center. Stir in undrained pineapple and vanilla until dry ingredients are just moistened and forms ball.

- **Knead** dough gently 10 to 12 times on lightly floured surface. Pat dough to ½-inch thickness. Cut with floured 2½-inch biscuit cutter.

- **Place** on baking sheet, sprayed with nonstick vegetable cooking spray. Brush tops with milk or cream.

- **Combine** almonds, remaining 1 tablespoon sugar and cinnamon. Sprinkle evenly over tops of scones. Bake at 400°F., 12 to 15 minutes. Serve warm.

Makes 12 scones

Per Serving: 159 calories, 6g fat (3g sat.), 9mg cholesterol, 295mg sodium, 25g carbohydrate (1g dietary fiber, 8g sugars), 3g protein, 4% Vit A, 4% Vit C, 4% calcium, 8% iron, 1% potassium, 8% folate

BREAKFAST

7

Pineapple Coffee Cake

Prep: 20 min.   Bake: 25 min.

1 can (20 oz.) DOLE
Pineapple Chunks
½ cup packed brown sugar
1 teaspoon ground cinnamon
½ cup chopped walnuts

3 tablespoons butter **or**
margarine, diced
2 cups prepared baking mix
2 tablespoons granulated
sugar
1 egg

- **Drain** pineapple, reserve ⅔ cup juice. Pat pineapple dry.

- **Mix** brown sugar, cinnamon, walnuts and butter in medium bowl; set aside.

- **Beat** reserved juice with baking mix, granulated sugar and egg in large bowl for 30 seconds. Spoon into 9-inch round baking pan sprayed with nonstick vegetable cooking spray. Top with half of walnut mixture, pineapple and remaining walnut mixture.

- **Bake** at 400° F., 20 to 25 minutes. Cool.

Makes 8 servings

Per Serving: 316 calories, 14g fat (4g sat.), 38mg cholesterol, 422mg sodium, 45g carbohydrate (1g dietary fiber, 25g sugars), 5g protein, 3% Vit A, 15% Vit C, 5% calcium, 10% iron, 4% potassium, 9% folate

Sunrise Pizza

Prep: 15 min.

2 DOLE Bananas, peeled
4 frozen whole wheat waffles
¼ cup low-fat whipped cream cheese
1 can (11 oz.) DOLE Mandarin Oranges, drained

2 teaspoons honey
Dash ground cinnamon
DOLE Fresh or Frozen Raspberries **or** Blueberries (optional)

- **Thinly** slice bananas on diagonal.
- **Prepare** waffles according to package directions.
- **Spread** waffles with cream cheese. Arrange banana slices on top, overlapping. Arrange mandarin oranges in center of each pizza. Drizzle with honey. Sprinkle with cinnamon. Garnish with raspberries or blueberries, if desired.

Makes 4 servings

Per Serving: 180 calories, 3g fat (1g sat.), 0mg cholesterol, 273mg sodium, 38g carbohydrate (2g dietary fiber, 19g sugars), 2g protein, 18% Vit A, 23% Vit C, 2% calcium, 12% iron, 7% potassium, 9% folate

Hawaiian Breakfast Wrap

Prep: 15 min.

6 eggs
¼ cup milk **or** water
¼ cup chopped ham **or** Canadian bacon
¼ cup chopped red **or** green bell pepper

2 tablespoons butter **or** margarine
1 can (8 oz.) DOLE Crushed Pineapple, drained
4 (8-inch) flour tortillas

• **Beat** together eggs and milk in medium bowl until blended. Set aside.

• **Cook** ham and bell pepper in hot butter over medium heat in large nonstick skillet until ham is lightly browned and pepper is tender-crisp. Stir in egg mixture and crushed pineapple. Scramble until desired doneness, stirring constantly.

• **Evenly** divide egg mixture onto flour tortillas. Roll sides up. Serve with watermelon wedges and lime slice, if desired.

Variation: Place mixture on toasted English muffins to serve as a sandwich.

Makes 4 servings

Per Serving: 262 calories, 16g fat (4g sat.), 324mg cholesterol, 365mg sodium, 17g carbohydrate (1g dietary fiber, 7g sugars), 13g protein, 19% Vit A, 36% Vit C, 9% calcium, 12% iron, 7% potassium, 14% folate

Yogurt Crunch Parfaits

Prep: 5 min.

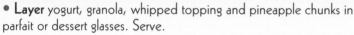

1 container (8 oz.) strawberry
yogurt **or** any flavor

1 cup granola **or** banana nut
crunch cereal

1 tub (8 oz.) COOL WHIP
Lite Whipped Topping,
thawed

1 can (20 oz.) DOLE
Pineapple Chunks, drained

• **Layer** yogurt, granola, whipped topping and pineapple chunks in parfait or dessert glasses. Serve.

Makes 6 servings

Per Serving: 307 calories, 11g fat (7g sat.), 1mg cholesterol, 28mg sodium, 43g carbohydrate (3g dietary fiber, 26g sugars), 5g protein, 0% Vit A, 25% Vit C, 8% calcium, 6% iron, 3% potassium, 4% folate

BREAKFAST

Hawaiian Bread

Prep: 20 min.   Bake: 50 min.

½ cup sugar
¼ cup butter **or** margarine, softened
2 eggs
1 can (8 oz.) DOLE Crushed Pineapple, undrained

⅓ cup chopped macadamia nuts **or** walnuts
1 cup flaked coconut, divided
2 cups prepared baking mix

- **Preheat** oven to 350°F.

- **Cream** sugar and butter in large bowl. Add eggs one at a time; beat well. Add undrained pineapple, nuts and ½ cup coconut and mix well. Stir in baking mix until just blended.

- **Pour** batter into 9 × 5-inch loaf pan, sprayed with nonstick vegetable cooking spray. Sprinkle and lightly press remaining ½ cup coconut into top of cake.

- **Bake** 50 minutes or until top is golden brown or toothpick inserted in center comes out clean.

- **Cool** in pan 10 minutes; remove from pan and cool slightly on wire rack. Serve warm.

Makes 12 servings

Per Serving: 240 calories, 14g fat (7g sat.), 45mg cholesterol, 318mg sodium, 28g carbohydrate (1g dietary fiber, 14g sugars), 4g protein, 3% Vit A, 4% Vit C, 3% calcium, 5% iron, 2% potassium, 6% folate

BREAKFAST

Honey Lime Fruit Toss

Prep: 10 min.

1 can (20 oz.) DOLE Pineapple Chunks
1 can (11 **or** 15 oz.) DOLE Mandarin Oranges, drained
1 large DOLE Banana, sliced
1 DOLE Kiwi fruit, peeled, halved and sliced

1 cup quartered DOLE Fresh **or** Frozen Strawberries
¼ teaspoon grated lime peel (optional)
2 tablespoons fresh lime juice
1 tablespoon honey

- **Drain** pineapple; reserve ¼ cup juice.
- **Combine** pineapple chunks, mandarin oranges, banana, kiwi fruit and strawberries in large serving bowl.
- **Stir** together reserved pineapple juice, lime peel, lime juice and honey in small bowl. Pour over salad; toss to coat.

Makes 7 servings

Per Serving: 103 calories, 0g fat (0g sat.), 0mg cholesterol, 3mg sodium, 26g carbohydrate (2g dietary fiber, 22g sugars), 1g protein, 5% Vit A, 62% Vit C, 2% calcium, 3% iron, 7% potassium, 3% folate

SALADS

Ambrosia

Prep: 15 min.

1 can (20 oz.) DOLE
   Pineapple Chunks, drained
1 can (11 **or** 15 oz.) DOLE
   Mandarin Oranges, drained
1 DOLE Banana, sliced

1½ cups seedless grapes
½ cup JET-PUFFED Miniature
   Marshmallows
1 cup vanilla low-fat yogurt
¼ cup flaked coconut, toasted

- **Combine** pineapple chunks, mandarin oranges, banana, grapes and marshmallows in medium bowl.
- **Stir** yogurt into fruit mixture. Sprinkle with coconut.

Makes 4 to 6 servings

Per Serving: 168 calories, 2g fat (2g sat.), 2mg cholesterol, 59mg sodium, 35g carbohydrate (2g dietary fiber, 30g sugars), 3g protein, 10% Vit A, 50% Vit C, 7% calcium, 3% iron, 8% potassium, 2% folate

Classic Mandarin Orange Salad

Prep: 15 min.

1 pkg. (5 oz.) DOLE Baby Spinach and Radicchio **or** other salad variety
1 can (15 oz.) DOLE Mandarin Oranges, drained
½ cup sliced carrots*

⅓ cup pecan halves, toasted
½ cup prepared light raspberry vinaigrette **or** raspberry walnut vinaigrette
¼ cup crumbled goat **or** feta cheese

• **Combine** spinach, mandarin oranges, carrots and pecans in large serving bowl.

• **Pour** dressing over salad; toss to evenly coat. Top with goat cheese.

*Note: Slice carrot with vegetable peeler in short lengthwise strips, if desired or cut crosswise into thin slices.

Makes 4 servings

Per Serving: 219 calories, 12 g fat (4 g sat.), 15 mg cholesterol, 132 mg sodium, 24 g carbohydrate (3 g dietary fiber, 16 g sugars), 7 g protein, 90% Vit A, 69% Vit C, 17% calcium, 8% iron, 8% potassium, 5% folate

SALADS

15

Asian Mandarin Salad

Prep: 15 min.

1 package (5 to 12 oz.)
DOLE Field Greens **or**
Chopped Romaine, **or** any
variety salad
⅓ cup crispy noodles
⅓ cup sliced almonds, toasted

1 can (11 **or** 15 oz.) DOLE
Mandarin Oranges, drained
½ cup bottled Asian sesame
dressing

• **Toss** together salad blend, noodles, almonds and mandarin oranges in large serving bowl. Pour dressing over salad; toss to evenly coat. Serve.

Makes 6 servings

Per Serving: 195 calories, 13g fat (1g sat.), 0mg cholesterol, 238mg sodium, 18g carbohydrate (2g dietary fiber, 14g sugars), 3g protein, 13% Vit A, 30% Vit C, 3% calcium, 4% iron, 3% potassium, 1% folate

SALADS

Festive Cranberry Pineapple Salad

Prep: 15 min.   Cook: 5 min.   Chill: 4 hr.

1 can (20 oz.) DOLE
  Crushed Pineapple, undrained
2 pkg. (4-serving size) **or**
  1 pkg. (8-serving size)
  JELL-O Raspberry **or**
  Cherry Flavored Gelatin

1 can (16 oz.) whole berry
  cranberry sauce
1 medium DOLE Apple,
  chopped
⅓ cup chopped walnuts

- **Drain** pineapple; reserve juice. Remove 1 tablespoon crushed pineapple; set aside for garnish. In medium saucepan, combine reserved juice with water to make 3 cups; heat to boiling. Add gelatin; stir at least 2 minutes until completely dissolved. Stir in cranberry sauce. Pour into large bowl. Refrigerate 1½ hours or until slightly thickened (consistency of unbeaten egg whites).

- **Stir** in remaining pineapple, apple and walnuts; stir gently until well blended. Pour into medium serving bowl.

- **Refrigerate** 4 hours or until firm. Garnish with reserved crushed pineapple and additional apple slices just before serving. Store leftover gelatin in refrigerator.

Makes 14 servings

Per Serving: 159 calories, 4g fat (0g sat.), 0mg cholesterol, 65mg sodium, 30g carbohydrate (1g dietary fiber, 27g sugars), 2g protein, 0% Vit A, 9% Vit C, 0% calcium, 2% iron, 2% potassium, 1% folate

SALADS

Watergate Salad

Prep: 15 min.   Refrigerate: 1 hr.

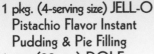

1 pkg. (4-serving size) JELL-O Pistachio Flavor Instant Pudding & Pie Filling
1 can (20 oz.) DOLE Crushed Pineapple, undrained

1 cup JET-PUFFED Miniature Marshmallows
½ cup chopped PLANTERS Pecans
1½ cups (½ of 8-oz. tub) thawed COOL WHIP Whipped Topping

- **Mix** dry pudding mix, pineapple, marshmallows and pecans in large bowl until well blended. Gently stir in whipped topping; cover.

- **Refrigerate** 1 hour or until ready to serve.

Makes 8 servings

Per Serving: 192 calories, 7g fat (3g sat.), 0mg cholesterol, 183 mg sodium, 29g carbohydrate (1g dietary fiber, 22g sugars), 1g protein, 0% Vit A, 15% Vit C, 0% calcium, 2% iron, 1% potassium, 0% folate

SALADS

Pineapple Apricot Glazed Ham

Prep: 20 min.   Bake: 1¾ hr.

1 can (20 oz.) DOLE
Pineapple Slices
1 (5½-pound) ham
Whole cloves
1 cup apricot jam **or** pineapple-
apricot jam, divided

2 tablespoons balsamic **or** red
wine vinegar
2 tablespoons honey
1 teaspoon cornstarch
⅛ teaspoon ground cinnamon

• **Drain** pineapple; reserve ¾ cup juice. Chop 4 pineapple slices into small pieces; set aside.

• **Score** top of ham in diamond pattern, making ¼-inch deep cuts. Insert cloves into each diamond. Place in shallow baking pan. Brush with ¼ cup jam; cover with foil.

• **Bake** ham according to package directions. Arrange 6 pineapple slices on top of ham during the last 30 minutes of baking. Brush pineapple and ham with another ¼ cup jam and continue baking.

• **Combine** reserved juice, vinegar, honey, cornstarch, cinnamon and remaining ½ cup jam in medium saucepan. Bring to boil. Reduce heat; cook and stir 2 minutes or until slightly thickened.

• **Stir** chopped pineapple into sauce; heat through. Serve warm over ham slices.

Makes 16 servings

Per Serving: 205 calories, 3g fat (1g sat.), 43mg cholesterol, 889mg sodium, 30g carbohydrate (1g dietary fiber, 22g sugars), 16g protein, 1% Vit A, 15% Vit C, 1% calcium, 6% iron, 8% potassium, 2% folate

ENTRÉES

Pork Chops with Pineapple Salsa

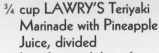

Prep: 15 min.   Marinate: 30 min.   Cook: 10 min.

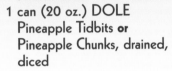

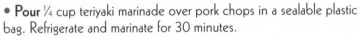

¾ cup LAWRY'S Teriyaki Marinade with Pineapple Juice, divided

4 boneless pork loin chops, ¾-inch thick

1 can (20 oz.) DOLE Pineapple Tidbits **or** Pineapple Chunks, drained, diced

⅓ cup finely chopped red onion

½ small red bell pepper, finely chopped

2 tablespoons chopped fresh cilantro

1 medium jalapeño pepper, seeded, finely chopped (optional)

- **Pour** ¼ cup teriyaki marinade over pork chops in a sealable plastic bag. Refrigerate and marinate for 30 minutes.

- **Combine** ¼ cup teriyaki marinade with pineapple chunks, red onion, bell pepper, cilantro and jalapeño pepper. Let stand at room temperature up to 1 hour.

- **Remove** pork chops from teriyaki marinade, discarding marinade. Grill or broil pork chops 10 to 15 minutes turning and brushing occasionally with remaining ¼ cup teriyaki marinade or until pork is no longer pink. Discard any remaining marinade. Serve chops with pineapple salsa.

Makes 4 servings

Per Serving: 233 calories, 2g fat (1g sat.), 51mg cholesterol, 2014mg sodium, 26g carbohydrate (2g dietary fiber, 22g sugars), 24g protein, 8% Vit A, 63% Vit C, 1% calcium, 6% iron, 14% potassium, 2% folate

Chipotle Shrimp & Pineapple Kabobs

Prep: 15 min.   Marinate: 30 min.   Cook: 8 min.

1 cup LAWRY'S Baja Chipotle Marinade with Lime Juice, divided
1½ pounds large shrimp, peeled and deveined

1 can (20 oz.) DOLE Pineapple Chunks, drained
1 medium red onion, cut into chunks
2 red **or** green bell peppers, cut into chunks

- **Pour** ¾ cup baja marinade over shrimp in large sealable plastic bag. Refrigerate and marinate for 30 minutes.

- **Remove** shrimp from baja marinade and plastic bag; discard marinade.

- **Thread** shrimp, pineapple chunks, onion and bell peppers onto skewers.

- **Grill** or broil 8 minutes turning and brushing with reserved baja marinade or until shrimp turns pink. Discard any remaining marinade.

Makes 4 to 6 servings

Per Serving: 280 calories, 6g fat (0g sat.), 265mg cholesterol, 316mg sodium, 26g carbohydrate (2g dietary fiber, 19g sugars), 29g protein, 35% Vit A, 190% Vit C, 6% calcium, 25% iron, 14% potassium, 5% folate

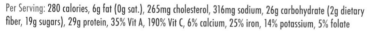

ENTRÉES

Citrus Teriyaki Chicken

Prep: 10 min.   Grill: 15 min.

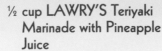

½ cup LAWRY'S Teriyaki
   Marinade with Pineapple
   Juice
1 teaspoon grated orange
   peel

1 teaspoon grated fresh ginger
5 boneless, skinless chicken
   breasts
1 can (20 oz.) DOLE
   Pineapple Slices

- **Stir** together teriyaki marinade, orange peel and ginger in small bowl.

- **Grill** or broil chicken breasts 8 minutes, brushing with one-half sauce. Turn chicken over; add pineapple slices to grill. Brush chicken and slices with remaining sauce. Continue grilling 8 to 10 minutes or until chicken is no longer pink in center and slices are lightly browned.

Makes 5 servings

Per Serving: 242 calories, 1g fat (1g sat.), 68mg cholesterol, 62mg sodium, 26g carbohydrate (1g dietary fiber, 24g sugars), 29g protein, 1% Vit A, 23% Vit C, 1% calcium, 7% iron, 9% potassium, 1% folate

ENTRÉES

Spicy Oriental Stir-Fry

Prep: 20 min.   Cook: 10 min.

1 can (20 oz.) DOLE
  Pineapple Chunks
½ cup ketchup
1 teaspoon sugar
1 teaspoon chili powder
1 teaspoon Worcestershire
  sauce
¼ teaspoon hot pepper sauce
2 tablespoons vegetable oil,
  divided

1 cup coarsely chopped green
  or red bell pepper*
1 cup snow peas*
1 pound boneless, skinless
  chicken breasts, cubed
¼ cup sliced DOLE Green
  Onions
  Hot cooked rice

- **Drain** pineapple; reserve 2 tablespoons juice.

- **Stir** together ketchup, reserved juice, sugar, chili powder, Worcestershire sauce and hot pepper sauce in bowl; set aside.

- **Heat** 1 tablespoon oil over medium-high heat in large skillet or wok. Add bell pepper; cook 1 to 2 minutes, stirring constantly. Add snow peas; cook 2 minutes more or until vegetables are tender-crisp. Remove vegetables from pan.

- **Add** remaining 1 tablespoon oil to skillet; add chicken. Cook 3 to 4 minutes or until chicken is no longer pink. Stir in reserved sauce, pineapple chunks, green onions and vegetables; heat until hot. Serve over rice.

*Tip: Substitute ½ package (16 oz.) frozen Oriental vegetable medley for bell peppers and snow peas, if desired. Add frozen vegetables in step 3 above; cook 3 to 4 minutes. Proceed as above.

Makes 4 servings

Per Serving: 358 calories, 11g fat (2g sat.), 96mg cholesterol, 457mg sodium, 28g carbohydrate (3g dietary fiber, 23g sugars), 37g protein, 18% Vit A, 92% Vit C, 5% calcium, 13% iron, 19% potassium, 7% folate

ENTRÉES

Hawaiian Chicken Sandwich

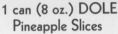

Prep: 10 min.   Marinate: 15 min.   Grill: 15 min.

1 can (8 oz.) DOLE Pineapple Slices
½ teaspoon dried oregano leaves, crushed
¼ teaspoon garlic powder
4 skinless, boneless, small chicken breast halves

½ cup light prepared Thousand Island salad dressing
¼ teaspoon ground red pepper (optional)
4 whole grain **or** whole wheat sandwich rolls
Red or green bell pepper, sliced into rings

- **Drain** pineapple; reserve juice.

- **Combine** reserved juice, oregano and garlic powder in medium bowl. Pour ¼ cup into shallow non-metallic dish. Add chicken breasts to dish; turn to coat both sides with marinade. Cover; marinate 15 minutes in refrigerator.

- **Add** pineapple slices to bowl; turn to coat both sides.

- **Grill** or broil chicken, brushing occasionally with reserved marinade, 8 minutes; turn over. Add pineapple slices to grill; continue cooking 8 to 10 minutes or until chicken is no longer pink in center and pineapple is golden brown. Discard any remaining marinade.

- **Combine** dressing and red pepper. Spread on bottom halves of rolls. Top with chicken, bell pepper rings, pineapple slices and top halves of rolls.

Makes 4 servings

Per Serving: 299 calories, 3g fat (1g sat.), 69mg cholesterol, 498mg sodium, 37g carbohydrate (4g dietary fiber, 19g sugars), 30g protein, 20% Vit A, 110% Vit C, 5% calcium, 10% iron, 13% potassium, 5% folate

ENTRÉES

Sweet 'n Sour

Prep: 15 min.   Cook: 15 min.

1 can (20 oz.) DOLE
  Pineapple Chunks
1 pound boneless, skinless
  chicken breasts
  Salt and black pepper to
  taste
1 tablespoon vegetable oil
2 DOLE Carrots, thinly sliced
1 green **or** red bell pepper,
  seeded, chunked

1 medium onion, chunked
1 clove garlic, minced
½ cup ketchup
⅓ cup packed brown sugar
1 tablespoon cornstarch
1 tablespoon soy sauce
1 teaspoon ground ginger
  Grated peel and juice from
  1 lemon
3 cups hot cooked rice

- **Drain** pineapple; reserve juice.

- **Cut** chicken into bite-size pieces. Season with salt and pepper. In large nonstick skillet, brown chicken in oil, in two batches, if necessary. Reduce heat. Add carrots, bell pepper, onion and garlic. Cover; simmer 5 minutes.

- **Combine** reserved juice, ketchup, brown sugar, cornstarch, soy sauce, ginger, lemon peel and lemon juice. Stir into skillet. Cover, simmer 5 minutes longer. Stir in pineapple until heated through. Serve with rice.

Makes 6 servings

Per Serving: 270 calories, 3g fat (0g sat.), 3mg cholesterol, 858mg sodium, 58g carbohydrate (3g dietary fiber, 29g sugars), 5g protein, 100% Vit A, 60% Vit C, 4% calcium, 4% iron, 6% potassium, 2% folate

ENTRÉES

Southwestern Pineapple and Chicken

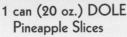

Prep: 5 min.   Marinate: 15 min.   Grill: 10 min.

1 can (20 oz.) DOLE
Pineapple Slices
1 tablespoon lime juice
1 tablespoon vegetable oil
1½ teaspoons chili powder

½ teaspoon dried oregano
leaves, crushed
1 garlic clove, finely chopped
5 boneless, skinless chicken
breast halves

- **Drain** pineapple; reserve ½ cup juice.

- **Combine** reserved pineapple juice, lime juice, oil, chili, oregano and garlic in sealable plastic bag. Add chicken. Refrigerate and marinate 15 minutes.

- **Grill** or broil chicken and pineapple, brushing occasionally with reserved marinade, 5 to 8 minutes on each side or until chicken is no longer pink in center and pineapple is lightly browned. Discard any remaining marinade.

Southwestern Pineapple and Fish: Substitute 2 pounds fish steaks such as halibut, swordfish **or** sea bass for chicken. Prepare recipe as directed except grill 8 to 10 minutes on each side or until fish flakes with a fork.

Makes 5 servings

Per Serving: 246 calories, 4g fat (1g sat.), 68mg cholesterol, 95mg sodium, 23g carbohydrate (1g dietary fiber, 20g sugars), 27g protein, 6% Vit A, 25% Vit C, 2% calcium, 8% iron, 9% potassium, 0% folate

ENTRÉES

Pineapple Teriyaki Chicken Kabobs

Prep: 15 min.   Grill: 15 min.

1 can (20 oz.) DOLE Pineapple Chunks
¾ cup LAWRY'S Teriyaki Marinade with Pineapple Juice
1 teaspoon Dijon-style mustard

4 (1½- to 1¾-pound) boneless, skinless chicken breasts cut into 1-inch pieces
2 red or green bell peppers, cut into 1½-inch pieces
1 zucchini cut into ½-inch-thick slices
12 wooden skewers (12 inches long) soaked in water

- **Drain** pineapple; reserve 2 tablespoons juice.

- **Combine** pineapple juice, teriyaki marinade and mustard. Set aside ¼ cup for grilling. Pour remaining marinade into sealable plastic bag; add chicken pieces, bell peppers and zucchini. Refrigerate and marinate for 30 minutes.

- **Remove** chicken and vegetables from plastic bag and discard marinade.

- **Thread** bell pepper, pineapple chunks, chicken and zucchini onto skewers. Brush with reserved marinade.

- **Grill** or broil 10 to 15 minutes, turning and brushing occasionally with teriyaki marinade, or until chicken is no longer pink. Discard any remaining marinade.

Makes 4 servings

Per Serving: 253 calories, 2g fat (1g sat.), 68mg cholesterol, 331mg sodium, 27g carbohydrate (3g dietary fiber, 22g sugars), 30g protein, 40% Vit A, 234% Vit C, 2% calcium, 9% iron, 16% potassium, 7% folate

ENTRÉES

27

Hawaiian Pizza Bites

Prep: 10 min.   Bake: 18 min.

1 canister (13.9 oz.)
  refrigerated pizza crust
  dough
¾ cup pizza sauce
1½ cups (6 oz.) shredded
  mozzarella cheese

3 oz. sliced Canadian bacon,
  cut into small pieces
1 can (8 oz.) DOLE
  Pineapple Tidbits **or**
1 can (20 oz.) DOLE
  Pineapple Chunks, drained

- **Unroll** dough onto lightly floured surface. Cut 15 to 16 circles with 3-inch cookie or biscuit cutter and place them on cookie sheet sprayed with nonstick vegetable cooking spray.

- **Bake** at 400°F., 8 minutes. Remove from oven. Top crusts with pizza sauce, one-half cheese, Canadian bacon and pineapple tidbits. Top with remaining cheese.

- **Bake** an additional 6 to 10 minutes or until crusts are golden brown.

Makes 15 to 16 pizza bites

Per Serving: 104 calories, 3g fat (0g sat.), 5mg cholesterol, 218mg sodium, 14g carbohydrate (1g dietary fiber, 2g sugars), 6g protein, 3% Vit A, 5% Vit C, 1% calcium, 1% iron, 1% potassium, 0% folate

Dole Sunrise Smoothie

Prep: 10 min.

1 cup DOLE Pineapple Juice
1 cup vanilla low-fat yogurt **or**
  frozen yogurt

1 cup DOLE Frozen
  Strawberries, partially
  thawed
2 ripe, medium DOLE
  Bananas, peeled

• **Combine** pineapple juice, yogurt, strawberries and bananas in blender or food processor container. Cover; blend until smooth. Garnish with strawberries and banana slices, if desired.

Makes 4 servings

Per Serving: 151 calories, 1g fat (1g sat.), 3mg cholesterol, 43mg sodium, 33g carbohydrate (3g dietary fiber, 27g sugars), 4g protein, 3% Vit A, 69% Vit C, 11% calcium, 2% iron, 8% potassium, 4% folate

BEVERAGES

Fruity Smoothie

Prep: 5 min.

1 ripe, large DOLE Banana, peeled
1 can (8 oz.) DOLE Pineapple Chunks, undrained

1 cup DOLE Frozen Mixed Berries **or** Blueberries, partially thawed
1 carton (8 oz.) blueberry **or** mixed berry yogurt

• **Slice** banana into blender or food processor container. Add pineapple chunks, mixed berries and yogurt. Cover; blend until smooth.

Variations: Replace 1 cup mixed berries and blueberry yogurt with:
Peach: 1 cup DOLE Frozen Sliced Peaches and peach yogurt
Raspberry: 1 cup DOLE Frozen Raspberries and mixed berry yogurt
Strawberries: 1 cup DOLE Frozen Strawberries and strawberry yogurt

Makes 3 servings

Per Serving: 160 calories, 1g fat (0g sat.), 4mg cholesterol, 66mg sodium, 36g carbohydrate (2g dietary fiber, 28g sugars), 3g protein, 1% Vit A, 38% Vit C, 10% calcium, 2% iron, 8% potassium, 2% folate

BEVERAGES

Easy Aloha Smoothie

Prep: 5 min.

1 can (15.25 oz.) DOLE
Tropical Mixed Fruit,
undrained

1 cup vanilla low-fat yogurt
1 cup ice cubes
Fresh mint sprigs (optional)

• **Combine** tropical mixed fruit, yogurt and ice cubes in blender or food processor container. Cover; blend until smooth. Garnish with mint sprigs, if desired.

Makes 3 servings

Per Serving: 164 calories, 1g fat (1g sat.), 4mg cholesterol, 66mg sodium, 35g carbohydrate (1g dietary fiber, 33g sugars), 4g protein, 1% Vit A, 1% Vit C, 14% calcium, 0% iron, 5% potassium, 2% folate

BEVERAGES

Pineapple-Mint Lemonade

Prep: 15 min.   Cook/Stand: 20 min.

1 cup sugar
⅔ cup water
⅓ cup chopped fresh mint

1 can (46 oz.) DOLE
   Pineapple Juice
1 cup lemon juice
   Fresh mint sprigs (optional)

- **Combine** sugar and water in large saucepan; bring to boil. Boil 1 minute; remove from heat.

- **Stir** in chopped mint; let stand 15 minutes.

- **Strain** liquid into punch bowl; discard chopped mint. Add pineapple and lemon juice. Serve over ice cubes in tall glasses. Garnish with mint sprigs, if desired.

Makes 8 servings

Per Serving: 162 calories, 0g fat (0g sat.), 0mg cholesterol, 8mg sodium, 42g carbohydrate (0g dietary fiber, 36g sugars), 0g protein, 8% Vit A, 96% Vit C, 0% calcium, 0% iron, 8% potassium, 0% folate

Summer Spritzer: Combine 2 cups Pineapple-Mint Lemonade with 2 cups mineral or sparkling water. Serve over ice. Makes 4 servings.

Creamy Pineapple Shake

Prep: 5 min.

1 can (20 oz.) DOLE
Crushed Pineapple,
undrained

1 pint vanilla ice cream **or**
frozen yogurt
1 cup milk
Dash ground cinnamon

• **Combine** crushed pineapple, ice cream, milk and cinnamon in blender or food processor container. Cover; blend until smooth.

Makes 4 servings

Per Serving: 210 calories, 4g fat (3g sat.), 15mg cholesterol, 90mg sodium, 37g carbohydrate (1g dietary fiber, 33g sugars), 5g protein, 8% Vit A, 29% Vit C, 17% calcium, 3% iron, 2% potassium, 1% folate

Pineapple Cranberry Punch

Prep: 5 min.

1 can (46 oz.) DOLE Pineapple Juice, chilled
1 bottle (32 oz.) cranberry juice cocktail, chilled
1 bottle (1 liter or 33.8 oz.) ginger ale, chilled

1 can (6 oz.) frozen orange juice concentrate, thawed*
Ice cubes
Garnish: orange slices, strawberry halves and mint sprigs

- **Combine** all ingredients in a punch bowl. Add ice cubes.
- **Garnish** with orange slices, strawberries or mint, as desired.

*Note: Can use ½ of 12-oz. can orange juice concentrate.

Makes 3½ quarts

Per Serving: 130 calories, 0g fat (0g sat.), 0mg cholesterol, 17mg sodium, 32g carbohydrate (0g dietary fiber, 28g sugars), 0g protein, 4% Vit A, 70% Vit C, 2% calcium, 1% iron, 8% potassium, 0% folate

Hot Spiced Pineapple Tea

Prep: 10 min.

1 can (46 oz.) DOLE
   Pineapple Juice
¼ cup honey

2 cinnamon sticks, broken
2 peppermint tea **or** mint
   medley herb tea bags

• **Combine** pineapple juice, honey and cinnamon in large saucepan. Bring to boil for 1 minute. Add tea bags, steep 2 to 5 minutes. Discard tea bags.

Makes 6 servings

Per Serving: 168 calories, 0g fat (0g sat.), 0mg cholesterol, 10mg sodium, 40g carbohydrate (0g dietary fiber, 35g sugars), 0g protein, 10% Vit A, 96% Vit C, 0% calcium, 0% iron, 9% potassium, 0% folate

BEVERAGES

Tropical Smoothie Punch

Prep: 15 min.

1 can (46 oz.) DOLE Pineapple Juice, chilled, divided

1 package (12 oz.) DOLE Frozen Raspberries, partially thawed, divided

4 cups **or** 1 liter sugar-free lemon-lime soda

½ (12-oz.) can frozen limeade concentrate, thawed

1 package (16 oz.) DOLE Frozen Sliced Peaches, partially thawed

2 DOLE Bananas, peeled, sliced

2 oranges, peeled, sliced

- **Combine** 1½ cups pineapple juice and ½ of the raspberries in blender container. Cover; blend until smooth.
- **Combine** all ingredients in punch bowl. Stir to combine.

Makes 25 (6-oz.) servings

Per Serving: 73 calories, 0g fat (0g sat.), 0mg cholesterol, 7mg sodium, 18g carbohydrate (1g dietary fiber, 14g sugars), 1g protein, 4% Vit A, 34% Vit C, 3% calcium, 1% iron, 3% potassium, 1% folate

BEVERAGES

Angel Lush with Pineapple

Prep: 15 min.   Chill: 1 hr.

1 can (20 oz.) DOLE
Crushed Pineapple,
undrained
1 pkg. (4-serving size)
JELL-O Vanilla Flavor
Instant Pudding & Pie Filling

1 cup thawed COOL WHIP
Whipped Topping
1 prepared angel food cake
Seasonal Berries

- **Mix** pineapple and pudding mix in medium bowl. Gently stir in whipped topping. Let stand 5 minutes.

- **Cut** cake horizontally into 3 layers. Place bottom cake layer, cut side up, on serving plate.

- **Spread** 1⅓ cups of the mixture onto cake layer; cover with middle cake layer. Spread 1 cup pudding onto middle cake layer; top with remaining cake layer. Spread with remaining pudding mixture. Refrigerate at least 1 hour or until ready to serve. Garnish with your favorite seasonal berries.

Makes 10 servings

Per Serving: 172 calories, 1g fat (1g sat.), 0mg cholesterol, 399mg sodium, 37g carbohydrate (1g dietary fiber, 14g sugars), 2g protein, 0% Vit A, 12 % Vit C, 5 % calcium, 2 % iron, 1% potassium, 3% folate

DESSERTS

Pineapple Upside-Down Minis

Prep: 20 min. Bake: 25 min.

2 cans (20 ounces each)
  DOLE Pineapple Slices
⅓ cup **butter or** margarine,
  melted
⅔ cup packed brown sugar

9 maraschino cherries,
  cut in half
1 package (18¼ ounces)
  yellow or pineapple-
  flavored cake mix

- **Drain** pineapple; reserve juice.

- **Stir** together melted butter and brown sugar. Evenly divide sugar mixture into 18 (⅔-cup) muffin cups, sprayed with nonstick vegetable cooking spray. Lightly press well-drained pineapple slices into sugar mixture. Place cherries in center of pineapple, sliced sides up.

- **Prepare** cake mix according to package directions, replacing amount of water called for with reserved juice. Pour ⅓ cup batter into each muffin cup.

- **Bake** at 350°F., for 20 to 25 minutes or until toothpick inserted in center comes out clean.

- **Cool** 5 minutes. Loosen edges and invert onto cookie sheets.

Makes 18 servings

Per Serving: 203 calories, 6g fat (2g sat.), 0mg cholesterol, 226mg sodium, 36g carbohydrate (1g dietary fiber, 28g sugars), 2g protein, 3% Vit A, 5% Vit C, 1% calcium, 3% iron, 1% potassium, 0% folate

DESSERTS

Lattice Pineapple Pie

Prep: 20 min.   Bake: 30 min.

1 can (20 oz.) DOLE
   Crushed Pineapple,
   undrained
½ cup sugar
2 tablespoons cornstarch
¼ teaspoon salt (optional)

1 tablespoon butter **or**
   margarine
1 tablespoon lemon juice
   Pastry for 9-inch double-
   crust pie

• **Combine** crushed pineapple, sugar, cornstarch and salt in saucepan. Cook, stirring, until thickened and clear. Stir in butter and lemon juice. Cool slightly.

• **Pour** filling into unbaked 9-inch pastry shell. Cut remaining pastry into 1-inch-wide strips for lattice top. Weave strips crisscross over pie to make lattice top. Pinch edges.

• **Bake** at 400°F., 25 to 30 minutes or until lightly golden brown.

Makes 8 servings

Per Serving: 336 calories, 16g fat (4g sat.), 4mg cholesterol, 316mg sodium, 45g carbohydrate (2g dietary fiber, 22g sugars), 3g protein, 1% Vit A, 13% Vit C, 2% calcium, 8% iron, 3% potassium, 9% folate

DESSERTS

Dole Golden Layer Cake

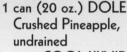

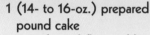

Prep: 20 min.   Chill: 30 min.

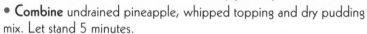

1 can (20 oz.) DOLE Crushed Pineapple, undrained
1½ cups COOL WHIP Whipped Topping, thawed
1 pkg. (4-serving size) JELL-O Instant Vanilla Flavor Pudding and Pie Filling Mix

1 (14- to 16-oz.) prepared pound cake
⅓ cup almond-flavored liqueur (or ⅓ cup pineapple juice and ½ teaspoon almond extract)
Sliced almonds, toasted (optional)
DOLE Pineapple Slices (optional)

• **Combine** undrained pineapple, whipped topping and dry pudding mix. Let stand 5 minutes.

• **Cut** cake lengthwise into thirds. Drizzle with liqueur. Spread one-third pudding mixture over bottom layer of cake. Top with second layer. Repeat layering, ending with pudding.

• **Chill** 30 minutes or overnight. Garnish with pineapple and sprinkle with toasted, sliced almonds, if desired.

Makes 12 servings

Per Serving: 228 calories, 8g fat (4g sat.), 22mg cholesterol, 234mg sodium, 35g carbohydrate (1g dietary fiber, 22g sugars), 2g protein, 1% Vit A, 8% Vit C, 1% calcium, 5% iron, 1% potassium, 0% folate

Mandarin Mousse Mold

Prep: 15 min.　Chill: 4½ hr.

1½ cups boiling water
1 pkg. (8-serving size) **or**
  2 pkg. (4-serving size)
  JELL-O Brand Orange **or**
  Mango Flavor Gelatin
1 cup cold water

1 can (11 **or** 15 oz.) DOLE
  Mandarin Oranges, drained
1 tub (8 oz.) COOL WHIP
  Whipped Topping, thawed,
  divided

- **Stir** boiling water into gelatin in large bowl 2 minutes until completely dissolved.

- **Stir** in cold water. Place mandarin oranges into 6-cup mold; spoon 2 cups gelatin mixture into mold over oranges. Refrigerate about 30 minutes or until set but not firm (should stick to finger and mound).

- **Meanwhile,** refrigerate remaining gelatin mixture about 30 minutes or until slightly thickened (consistency of unbeaten egg whites). Stir in 2 cups of the whipped topping with wire whisk until smooth. Pour over gelatin layer in mold.

- **Refrigerate** 4 hours or until firm. Unmold. Garnish with remaining whipped topping. Store leftover gelatin mold in refrigerator.

Unmolding: Dip mold in warm water for about 15 seconds. Gently pull gelatin from around edges with moist fingers. Place moistened serving plate on top of mold. Invert mold and plate; holding mold and plate together, shake slightly to loosen. Gently remove mold and center gelatin on plate.

Makes 12 servings

Per Serving: 122 calories, 3g fat (3g sat.),0mg cholesterol, 56mg sodium, 21g carbohydrate (0g dietary fiber, 19g sugars), 1g protein, 0% Vit A, 4% Vit C, 0% calcium, 1% iron, 0% potassium, 0% folate

DESSERTS

Easy Fruit Parfaits

Prep: 5 min.   Chill: 4 hr.

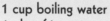

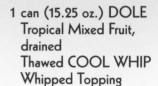

1 cup boiling water
1 pkg. (4-serving size)
   JELL-O Brand Gelatin, any
   red flavor
1 cup cold water

1 can (15.25 oz.) DOLE
Tropical Mixed Fruit,
drained
Thawed COOL WHIP
Whipped Topping

• **Stir** boiling water into gelatin in medium bowl 2 minutes until completely dissolved. Stir in cold water. Pour gelatin into 4 tall dessert or parfait glasses, filling about half full.

• **Refrigerate** 4 hours or until firm. To serve, layer with whipped topping and tropical mixed fruit.

Makes 4 servings

Per Serving: 177 calories, 2g fat (2g sat.), 0mg cholesterol, 108mg sodium, 39g carbohydrate (1g dietary fiber, 36g sugars), 2g protein, 0% Vit A, 0% Vit C, 0% calcium, 0% iron, 0% potassium, 0% folate

Toasted Pecan-Pineapple Sauce

Prep: 10 min.　Cook: 5 min.

1 can (20 oz.) DOLE
　Pineapple Chunks
½ cup orange juice
2 teaspoons cornstarch
1 tablespoon sugar
½ teaspoon ground ginger

½ teaspoon grated orange
　peel (optional)
¼ cup chopped pecans,
　toasted
¼ cup toasted coconut

- **Drain** pineapple; reserve ½ cup juice.

- **Stir** together orange juice, reserve juice, cornstarch, sugar, ginger and orange peel. Stir in pineapple chunks. Cook until sauce begins to boil and thickens slightly.

- **Stir** in pecans and coconut. Serve over ice cream, angel food cake or pound cake.

Makes 8 servings

Per Serving: 93 calories, 5g fat (2g sat.), 0mg cholesterol, 9mg sodium, 13g carbohydrate (1g dietary fiber, 10g sugars), 1g protein, 3% Vit A, 24% Vit C, 0% calcium, 2% iron, 1% potassium, 0% folate

DESSERTS

Pineapple Oatmeal Cookies

Prep: 20 min.   Bake: 25 min.

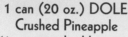

1 can (20 oz.) DOLE Crushed Pineapple
1½ cups packed brown sugar
1 cup butter **or** margarine, softened
1 egg
3 cups old fashioned **or** quick cooking oats

2 cups all-purpose flour
1 teaspoon baking powder
1 teaspoon ground cinnamon
½ teaspoon salt
1 cup DOLE Seedless **or** Golden Raisins
1 cup chopped almonds, toasted (optional)

- **Drain** pineapple well; reserve ½ cup juice.

- **Beat** sugar and butter until light and fluffy in large bowl. Beat in egg, crushed pineapple and reserved juice.

- **Combine** oats, flour, baking powder, cinnamon, salt, raisins and almonds in medium bowl. Stir into pineapple mixture.

- **Drop** by heaping tablespoonfuls onto greased cookie sheets. Shape with back of spoon.

- **Bake** at 350°F., 20 to 25 minutes or until golden. Cool on wire racks.

Makes about 4 dozen

Per Serving: 336 calories, 11g fat (5g sat.), 25mg cholesterol, 175mg sodium, 49g carbohydrate (3g dietary fiber, 31g sugars), 7g protein, 4% Vit A, 6% Vit C, 4% calcium, 13% iron, 5% potassium, 6% folate

DESSERTS

Polynesian Sunshine Pie

Prep: 15 min.   Chill: 1 hr.

1 can (15 oz.) DOLE
 Mandarin Oranges
1 graham cracker crust (6 oz.)
1 DOLE Banana, sliced
6 oz. (¾ of 8-oz. pkg.) cream
 cheese, softened
1 teaspoon vanilla extract

1 tub (8 oz.) COOL WHIP
 Whipped Topping, thawed
⅔ cup flaked coconut,
 toasted, divided
1 can (15.25 oz.) DOLE
 Tropical Mixed Fruit,
 drained
⅓ cup apricot jam, melted

• **Drain** oranges; reserve 2 tablespoons syrup. Place half of the oranges in bottom of crust. Top with half of the banana slices; set aside.

• **Beat** cream cheese, reserved syrup and vanilla until well blended. Gently stir in whipped topping. Stir in ⅓ cup coconut. Spread mixture over fruit in crust. Refrigerate at least 1 hour.

• **Arrange** tropical mixed fruit, banana slices and remaining mandarin oranges over filling. Drizzle jam over fruit. Sprinkle remaining coconut over pie.

Makes 1 (9-inch) pie

Per Serving: 423 calories, 23g fat (15g sat.), 23mg cholesterol, 165mg sodium, 29g carbohydrate (2g dietary fiber, 30g sugars), 4g protein, 15% Vit A, 54% Vit C, 3% calcium, 8% iron, 3% potassium, 2% folate

DESSERTS

Easy Pineapple Citrus Layered Cake

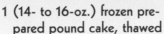

Prep: 20 min.   Chill: 1 hr.

1 (14- to 16-oz.) frozen prepared pound cake, thawed
1 package (8 oz.) cream cheese, softened
1 cup powdered sugar
1 tablespoon grated orange peel
1 tablespoon orange juice

¾ teaspoon almond **or** vanilla extract
1 can (20 oz.) DOLE Crushed Pineapple, well drained
Sliced almonds, toasted (optional)

- **Slice** pound cake horizontally into thirds; set aside.

- **Beat** together cream cheese, sugar, orange peel, orange juice and almond extract in large bowl until smooth and blended. Stir in pineapple.

- **Place** bottom cake layer on serving platter, spread with one-third of pineapple mixture over cake. Repeat layers ending with pineapple mixture. Chill at least 1 hour or overnight before serving. Sprinkle with almonds, if desired.

Makes 10 servings

Per Serving: 334 calories, 15g fat (7g sat.), 49mg cholesterol, 208mg sodium, 47g carbohydrate (1g dietary fiber, 33g sugars), 4g protein, 7% Vit A, 10% Vit C, 4% calcium, 7% iron, 2% potassium, 1% folate

DESSERTS